BURMESE PYTHON VS. SUN BEAR

BY NATHAN SOMMER

BELLWETHER MEDIA • MINNEAPOLIS, MN

Torque brims with excitement
perfect for thrill-seekers of all kinds.
Discover daring survival skills, explore
uncharted worlds, and marvel at mighty
engines and extreme sports. In *Torque* books,
anything can happen. Are you ready?

This edition first published in 2024 by Bellwether Media, Inc.

No part of this publication may be reproduced in whole or in part without written
permission of the publisher. For information regarding permission, write to
Bellwether Media, Inc., Attention: Permissions Department,
6012 Blue Circle Drive, Minnetonka, MN 55343.

Library of Congress Cataloging-in-Publication Data

LC record for Burmese Python vs. Sun Bear available at:
https://lccn.loc.gov/2023000645

Editor: Kieran Downs   Designer: Josh Brink

Printed in the United States of America, North Mankato, MN.

TABLE OF CONTENTS

THE COMPETITORS

Many different animals call the **rain forests** of Southeast Asia home. Burmese pythons are some of the strongest **predators** among them. These **reptiles** take down **prey** that is much larger than them.

Sun bears are ready to battle! These bears will attack any challenger. What happens when these two animals meet?

5

Burmese pythons are often brought to the United States to be pets. But they can be hard to care for. Many people illegally release them. The snakes have become an invasive species in Florida.

Burmese pythons are some of the world's largest snakes. They grow up to 23 feet (7 meters) long. They can weigh up to 200 pounds (90.7 kilograms).

These **constrictors** have thick bodies and tan skin with dark brown markings. They are **native** to the rain forests and marshes of Southeast Asia.

BURMESE PYTHON PROFILE

LENGTH
UP TO 23 FEET
(7 METERS)

WEIGHT
UP TO 200 POUNDS
(90.7 KILOGRAMS)

0   6 FEET   12 FEET   18 FEET   24 FEET

HABITAT

RAIN FORESTS   MARSHES   WETLANDS

BURMESE PYTHON RANGE

■ RANGE

SUN BEAR PROFILE

LENGTH
**UP TO 5 FEET
(1.5 METERS)**

WEIGHT
**UP TO 176 POUNDS
(80 KILOGRAMS)**

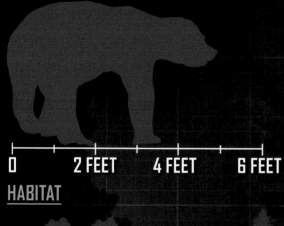

| 0 | 2 FEET | 4 FEET | 6 FEET |

HABITAT

RAIN FORESTS

SWAMPS

SUN BEAR RANGE

☐ **RANGE**

Sun bears are the world's smallest **species** of bear. They grow up to 5 feet (1.5 meters) long and weigh up to 176 pounds (80 kilograms).

Sun bears have small ears, short **muzzles**, and long tongues. They are named after the gold markings on their chests. The bears are found throughout the rain forests and swamps of Southeast Asia.

LONG TONGUES

Sun bear tongues can grow up to 10 inches (25.4 centimeters) long!

SECRET WEAPONS

Burmese pythons have razor-sharp teeth. Their top jaws have two rows of teeth. Their bottom jaws have one row. Their teeth curve inward to keep prey in their mouths.

Sun bears pack a powerful bite. Their strong jaws and large **canine teeth** bite into trees to find insects underneath the bark. Their jaws and teeth are also useful against enemies!

SIZE COMPARISON

BURMESE PYTHON
23 FEET (7 METERS)

0	5 FEET	10 FEET	15 FEET	20 FEET	25 FEET

PICKUP TRUCK
20 FEET (6.1 METERS)

0	5 FEET	10 FEET	15 FEET	20 FEET	25 FEET

ALLIGATOR EATERS

Large pythons have been seen attacking and eating alligators!

After capturing prey with their teeth, Burmese pythons **unhinge** their jaws. Stretchy **ligaments** in their jaws allow them to open wide. The snakes can swallow prey five times wider than their heads!

Sun bears have loose skin. This allows them to twist and turn when they are grabbed. They easily escape from their enemies.

SECRET WEAPONS

SHARP TEETH

WIDE JAWS

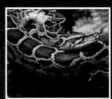

LONG, STRONG BODIES

Burmese pythons have long, strong bodies.
They wrap them around prey and squeeze tightly.
They squeeze until their prey stops breathing!

SECRET WEAPONS

SUN BEAR

STRONG JAWS

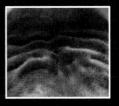
LOOSE SKIN

SHARP CLAWS

SUN BEAR CLAW

UP TO 4 INCHES
(10.2 CENTIMETERS)

Sun bears have sharp claws. They grow up to 4 inches (10.2 centimeters) long. They use these to tear into trees and dig for food. The claws can also hurt attackers.

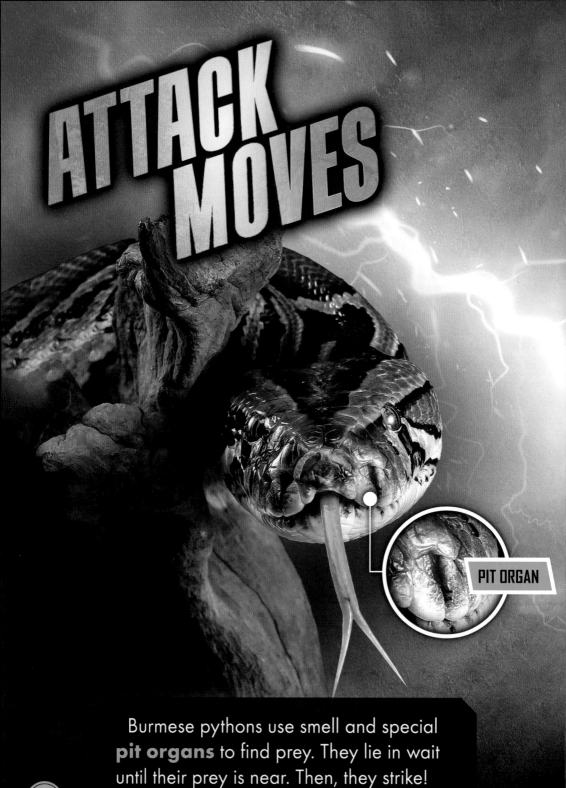

ATTACK MOVES

PIT ORGAN

Burmese pythons use smell and special **pit organs** to find prey. They lie in wait until their prey is near. Then, they strike!

Sun bears fight when threatened. Females become **aggressive** when protecting their cubs. They growl and roar to let enemies know they are going to fight.

Burmese pythons strike using their sharp teeth. This traps prey in their wide jaws. The snakes coil around their trapped prey. They squeeze until it cannot breathe. Then, they swallow their meal whole.

Sun bears **slash** at enemies with their claws. The bears twist around in their loose skin when they are grabbed. This helps them bite their enemies!

LIFE IN THE TREES

Sun bears spend a lot of their time in trees. Some even make their beds in trees!

19

READY, FIGHT!

A Burmese python watches a sun bear cub. It prepares to **ambush**. The cub gets closer. The python strikes! Its teeth sink into the cub.

The mother sun bear runs over. It claws the python. The snake lets go and slithers away. Nothing attacks the mother's cub without a fight!

GLOSSARY

aggressive—ready to fight

ambush—to carry out a surprise attack

canine teeth—long, pointed teeth that are often the sharpest in the mouth

constrictors—snakes that use their bodies to squeeze prey

ligaments—tough pieces of tissue that connect bones

muzzles—the noses and mouths of some animals

native—originally from the area

pit organs—special body parts that allow snakes to detect the movements of prey in darkness

predators—animals that hunt other animals for food

prey—animals that are hunted by other animals for food

rain forests—thick, green forests that receive a lot of rain

reptiles—cold-blooded animals that have backbones and lay eggs

slash—to cut with a sharp object

species—kinds of animals

unhinge—to open wider than the bones would normally allow

TO LEARN MORE

AT THE LIBRARY

Davies, Monika. *Deadly Pythons*. New York, N.Y.: Gareth Stevens Publishing, 2023.

Huddleston, Emma. *Burmese Pythons*. Lake Elmo, Minn.: Focus Readers, 2022.

Sommer, Nathan. *Siberian Tiger vs. Brown Bear*. Minneapolis, Minn.: Bellwether Media, 2021.

ON THE WEB

FACTSURFER

Factsurfer.com gives you a safe, fun way to find more information.

1. Go to www.factsurfer.com

2. Enter "Burmese python vs. sun bear" into the search box and click Q.

3. Select your book cover to see a list of related content.

INDEX